Day Trading Options

Most Complete Course for Beginners With Strategies and Techniques of Day Trading for Living

Mark Robert Rich

© **Copyright 2020 Mark Robert Rich - All rights reserved.**

The content contained within this book may not be reproduced, duplicated or transmitted without direct written permission from the author or the publisher.

Under no circumstances will any blame or legal responsibility be held against the publisher, or author, for any damages, reparation, or monetary loss due to the information contained within this book. Either directly or indirectly.

Legal Notice:

This book is copyright protected. This book is only for personal use. You cannot amend, distribute, sell, use, quote or paraphrase any part, or the content within this book, without the consent of the author or publisher.

Disclaimer Notice:

Please note the information contained within this document is for educational and entertainment purposes only. All effort has been executed to present accurate, up to date, and reliable, complete information. No warranties of any kind are declared or implied. Readers acknowledge that the author is not engaging in the rendering of legal, financial, medical or professional advice. The content within this book has been derived from various sources. Please consult a licensed professional before attempting any techniques outlined in this book.

By reading this document, the reader agrees that under no circumstances is the author responsible for any losses, direct or indirect, which are incurred as a result of the use of information contained within this document, including, but not limited to, — errors, omissions, or inaccuracies.

Table of Contents

INTRODUCTION 9
    THE BENEFITS OF DAY TRADING OPTIONS 10
    WHAT YOU WILL LEARN IN THIS BOOK 12

CHAPTER 1: OPTIONS BASICS 15
    WHAT ARE OPTIONS? 15
    TYPES OF OPTIONS 18
        Call Options *18*
        Put Options *19*
    GOING LONG VS. GOING SHORT 20
    OPTION PREMIUM PRICES 21
    TRADING OPTIONS BENEFITS 24
    TRADING OPTIONS DISADVANTAGES 25
    CHAPTER SUMMARY 26

CHAPTER 2: DAY TRADING OPTIONS BASICS 28
    WHAT OPTIONS DAY TRADERS DO 28
    HOW TO GET STARTED AS AN OPTIONS DAY TRADER 30
    PLANNING FOR SUCCESS 31
        Your Goals *32*
        Entry Into the Options Trading Market *33*
        An Efficient Workspace *33*
        Developing a Time Schedule *33*
        Personal Development *34*
    THE QUALITIES OF AN EFFECTIVE OPTIONS DAY TRADER 34

CHAPTER SUMMARY 37

CHAPTER 3: THE TRADING MARKET 38

DECIDING WHAT MARKET TO TRADE-IN 38
HOW TO FIND THE BEST OPTIONS TO DAY TRADE 40
    Technical Analysis 40
    Price Charts 41
    Line Charts 41
    Open-High-Low-Close Bar Chart 42
    Candlestick Chart 43
FACTORS THAT AFFECT THE OPTIONS MARKET 45
CHAPTER SUMMARY 45

CHAPTER 4: OPTIONS DAY TRADING STYLES 47

BREAKOUT OPTIONS DAY TRADING 48
MOMENTUM OPTIONS DAY TRADING 50
REVERSAL OPTIONS DAY TRADING 51
SCALPING OPTIONS DAY TRADING 51
USING PIVOT POINTS FOR OPTIONS DAY TRADING 53
CHAPTER SUMMARY 55

CHAPTER 5: TRADING OPTIONS STRATEGIES EVERY DAY TRADER SHOULD KNOW 58

COVERED CALL STRATEGY 58
CREDIT SPREADS 60
DEBIT SPREADS. 61
IRON CONDOR 63
ROLLING OUT OPTIONS 64
ROLLING CAN BE DONE IN 3 WAYS. THEY ARE: 64
STRADDLE STRATEGY 65

Strangle Strategy 65
Chapter Summary 66

CHAPTER 6: POWER PRINCIPLES TO ENSURE A STRONG ENTRY INTO DAY TRADING OPTIONS 69

Power Principle #1 – Ensure Good Money Management 69
    Money Management Tips for Options Traders 70
Power Principle #2 – Ensure That Risks and Rewards Are Balanced 72
Power Principle #3 – Develop a Consistent Monthly Options Trading System 73
Power Principle #4 – Consider a Brokerage Firm That is Right for Your Level of Options Expertise 75
    Broker Cash and Margin Accounts 76
    Broker Services and Features 76
    Commissions and Other Fees 77
    Broker Reputation and Options Expertise 78
Power Principle #5 – Ensure That Exits Are automated 79
Chapter Summary 79

CHAPTER 7: 11 OPTIONS DAY TRADING RULES FOR SUCCESS 81

The Rule for Success #1 – Have Realistic Expectations 82
The Rule for Success #2 – Start Small to Grow a Big Portfolio 83
The Rule for Success #3 – Know Your Limits 83
The Rule for Success #4 – Be Mentally, Physically and Emotionally Prepared Every Day 84
The Rule for Success #5 – Do Your Homework Daily 85
The Rule for Success #6 – Analyze Your Daily Performance 86
The Rule for Success #7 – Do Not Be Greedy 87
The Rule for Success #8 – Pay Attention to Volatility 87
The Rule for Success #9 – Use the Greeks 88

  Delta *88*

  Vega *89*

  Theta *89*

  Gamma *89*

  Rho *90*

 The Rule for Success #10 – Be Flexible 90

 The Rule for Success #11 – Have an Accountability Partner or Mentorship 90

 Chapter Summary 91

CONCLUSION 93

 Characteristics of a Successful Options Day Trader 94

 Final Words 95

Introduction

Are you looking for a high-stakes career that always has something new to offer? Perhaps you are looking for a challenge or a way to benefit from your analytical mind? Or maybe you want to earn a limitless income from a growing and resilient industry?

If you answered yes to even just one of these questions, then it is time that you consider a career in options trading. Let's face it. We live in a world where job security is no longer existent. People are being laid off and fired at the drop of a hat, even days before retirement. Job markets crash all the time and businesses go out of business unexpectedly. It is a terrible thing to have the rug pulled out from under you in such circumstances, but be aware of the possibility that it could happen allows you to be prepared and to ensure that you are not left adrift if this does indeed come to pass.

The solution is to create wealth that does not depend on other people or someone else's business. Your destiny needs to be solely in your hands. This means becoming your own boss.

Trading options offers that opportunity for entrepreneurship. Not only that. It offers strategies and systems that are proven to be successful, sustainable and lucrative. You do not have to reinvent the wheel. The wheel is already invented with options trading. You just have to get in the driver's seat and take off on your individual journey.

Day trading options gives you control of your income and your time. You can learn what works and what does not in as little as one day. That is the nature of day trading options. It moves fast. Results are seen within hours. You can discard and adopt strategies fast. How many careers can you say allows you to see huge results in so little time? You do not have to wait months — or worse, years — to know what works for you.

I can personally attest to the wonders that this career has made in my life. I was struggling to get by at one time. I was behind on the bills and down on my luck. I was on the verge of hitting rock bottom, but that was precisely where I was meant to be because desperation sent me searching for a solution to my woes. My solution: Day Trading Options.

It was tough getting my feet wet at the beginning, but I stuck with it and I could not be happier for the benefits I gained.

The Benefits of Day Trading Options

Here are just a few of the advantages that a day trading option has allowed me:

- **Affordability**: Stocks and mutual funds are items worth investing in, but they can be pricey to purchase. Trading options allowed me to enter that market without buying such assets outright. This was done at a significantly lower cost and still afforded me the benefits of being in the business.
- **No obligation**. I did not have to buy or sell anything unless it benefited me to do so. The risk was significantly lower compared to owning the assets associated with options.
- **Diverse portfolio**. Because I do not have to buy actual assets, I can dabble in several investment opportunities at once to see what works for me and what does not. I can use the capital that I do have to increase my profit rather than worry about increasing the worth of all these assets.
- **Gaining increased profit from assets that I do own**. Day trading options allows me to leverage the assets that I do own and gain income from them.
- **Longevity**. Trading ptions is a part of the financial market that is amazingly resilient and can even thrive in volatile situations.

Day trading options is not something that is a one-size-fits-all. Different people have different experiences with them. I believe it takes a special kind of person to put in the work, time, effort, and dedication that is needed to be a successful options day trader. Only you can answer whether or not you have got the right stuff for this career. This book was written to help you figure that out.

What You Will Learn In This Book

This book is not a textbook nor is it written for professional options day traders. It was written to help someone who is new to options and day trading discover this exciting career and ultimately make a decision on whether or not this career is right for him or her to pursue.

This book is a comprehensive guide on:

- What options are?
- The types of options.
- How option premiums are priced.
- What it means to be an options day trader.
- How to get started as an options day trader.
- The ins and out of the trading market.
- The best day trading option strategies.
- The power principles every options day trader needs to know.
- The rules for success as an options day trader.

So much more!

The explanations in this book are straight-to-the-point with no fluff or unnecessary additives. Every word was written to create value on how to get started with options and day trading and how to create longevity with both.

Day trading options is a business. It is a venture that is made for someone who wants to start a new business or build their wealth by investing in new techniques that work in this modern global economy. It is not something that is made for playing. Either you make a serious commitment to master it or move onto something else that you can make that kind of commitment to. You need to be serious about using this as a tool to set up the kind of future you want, financially and otherwise. When day trading options is done right, it allows you to use your time the way you want rather than being chained to a desk all day or any other 9 to 5 job. If you want to travel the world and explore new cultures, then this career should be a serious consideration. If you want the freedom to dictate what you do with your time, then this career should be an option for you. If you want an income that far surpasses anything you can earn in the regular grind, then this career is for you.

But it will not just happen. You have to make this work for you, and that ability is what separates amateur options day traders and the professionals. This ability is not an obscure thing. It is attainable with persistence, consistency and dedication. Nothing is preventing you from capturing that success for yourself except you.

Turn the page to learn how day trading options can improve your life.

Chapter 1: Options Basics

Obviously, to become a master at day trading options, you need to master options itself. This chapter is dedicated to giving you the basics of what you need to know to master the concepts of options such as the basic types of options, the anatomy of an options contract, what it means to go long and go short and the benefits of trading options compared to other types of investments.

What are Options?

Stocks and options are often confused by persons who are not involved deeply in the financial market, but the two things have completely different characteristics. Stocks are a representation of ownership in individual companies. They can also be components of options.

Stocks are so popular because they represent a great investment opportunity for someone who is looking for a long-term profit yield and has the capital to invest. They are also a great investment tool for someone who would like to experience that steady growth in profit without having to keep a day-to-day eye on that investment.

As great as the investment in stocks is, it also comes with risks. The hope that an investor makes when investing in stocks is that the price or value will rise, so that he or she obtains profit from that increase. The nature of stocks is that they can rise and fall at any time, and an investor can completely lose his or her investment if stock prices plummet to zero, which can happen at the drop of a hat. Stocks are volatile entities from day to day because they are very reactive to world events such as natural disasters, wars, politics, and more. As a result, an investor needs to be very picky about how he or she chooses to invest in stocks, and even that is not a soundproof process because there is no telling what can happen with stocks.

Fortunately, there is a safety net that an investor can use to ensure that this loss is kept to a minimum while still being able to reap the benefits and profits of owning stocks and other types of assets. This safety net is called trading options.

In the most basic terms, an option is a financial contract. Its main purpose is to facilitate the right to buy or sell an asset that is associated with the contract by a certain date at a specific price. The person who obtains this right is known as the holder or the investor of the contract. The person who sells this contract is known as the seller.

The contract is called an option because the holder of the contract is under no obligation to exercise this right by the date specified. This specified date is known as the expiration date. The asset associated with such a contract is typically stock, but this is not limited to that type of asset only. ETF, also known as Exchange-Traded Funds, indexes, currencies and even physical commodities, can be the asset associated with options.

More specifically, options are called derivative contracts because they derive their value based on the value of the asset attached to that contract. This means that the seller of the option does not have to own the associated asset. At the most basic, the seller just needs to have enough money to cover the price of that associated asset to fulfill that contract if the holder chooses to exercise the right to buy or sell. There are even situations where the seller will offer the holder of the contract another derivative contract in circumstances where this is easier to provide than the asset itself. This makes options a very versatile tool for both buyers and sellers.

The specific selling or buying price mentioned in the definition of an option is also called the strike price. It is so named because this is the price at which the trader will strike his or her right if the asset value moves in the direction that he or she would like. It remains the same for the length of the contract.

Types of Options

The two main types of options are called call options and put options. We will address the specifics of each type below.

Call Options

Most commonly just simply called a call, this type of option allows the trader of the option the right to buy the associated asset on or before the expiration date. The reason that anyone would be interested in buying the attached asset is that the price is expected to rise within the lifetime of the option. As a result, the profit lies in the price of the asset going above the strike price. The seller makes a profit from the trader paying him or her a premium for that option. In the event that the asset does rise in price, then the buyer of the option has the right to exercise the option to buy the asset or sell the option. Both strategies lead to a profit for the buyer. In this scenario, the buyer has the potential for unlimited income, while the seller's income is limited to the premium paid for that option.

The term that describes whether or not a trader has made a profit includes "in the money," "out of the money" and "at the money."

In the money, describes the situation whereby the asset price has gone above the strike price. This is favorable and describes a profitable situation for the trader. **Out of the**

money describes the situation whereby the asset price has fallen below the strike price resulting in a loss from the option. **At the money** means that the asset price is equivalent to the strike price and so the trader does not profit or lose from the option.

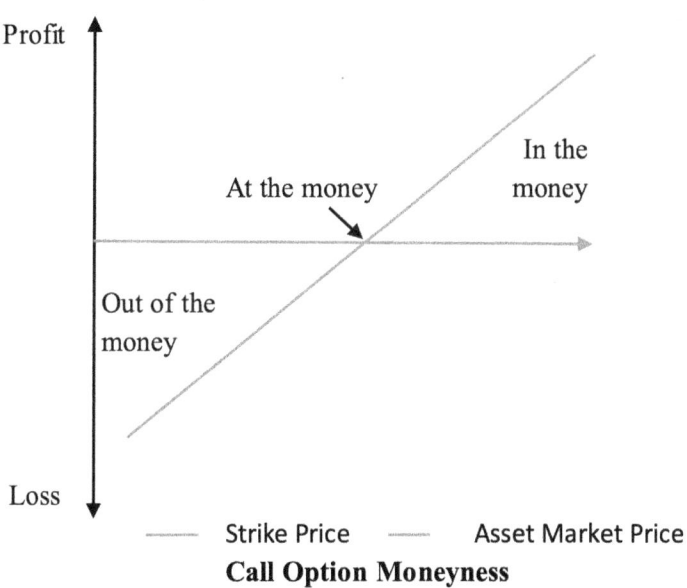

Call Option Moneyness

Put Options

Also commonly called a put, this type of option gives the trader the right to sell the asset attached to the contract at the strike price on or before the expiration date. Just like with a call option, the strike price is predetermined with this type of option. The trader is in the money when the price of the asset goes below the strike price of the option. Only if the price goes down does the trader to make a profit. If the asset price goes up, then the trader is out of the money and therefore, makes a loss. If the asset price is equivalent to the strike price by the time the expiration date rolls around, then the trader is at the money.

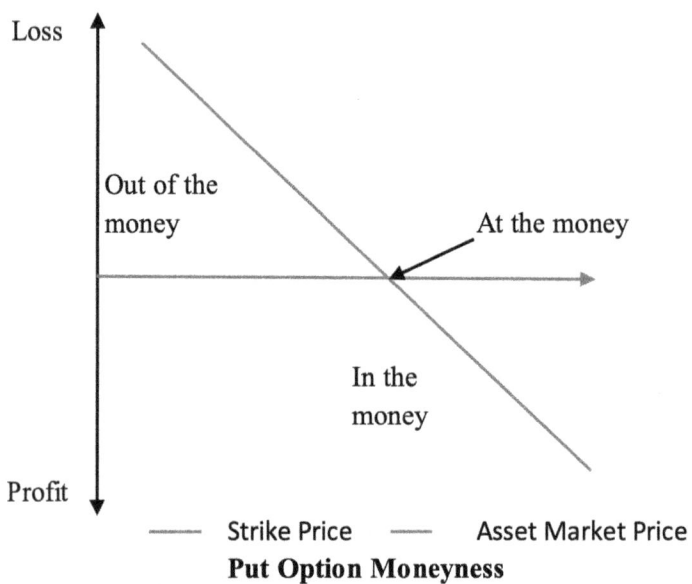

Put Option Moneyness

If the trader is in the money by the expiration date, he or she has the option to sell the asset associated with the option by a fixed time or sell the option to someone else.

Going Long vs. Going Short

While they are polar opposites, Going Long and Going Short both describe the state of ownership of the asset associated with the option. **Going short** is also known as having a short position. It describes the state of the seller, not owning the asset associated with the option. **Going long** is also described as having a long position. It means that the seller owns the asset associated with the option.

There is another application of long and short positions, and it applies to both call and put options. Having a long call option means that the trader expects the price of the asset to go up so that he or she can benefit. The opposite is true for having a long put option. The trader expects the price of the asset to depreciate, so that he or she can exercise the right to sell the option at the strike price.

As you can see, neither of these options refer to the time period associated with that option. Rather, the focus is on the ownership of the associated asset. As such, the person who owns the asset is called the long position holder. If this person expects the price of the asset to rise, then this is called having a bullish view. This applies to a trader holding a long call option.

If this person expects the price of the asset to fall, this is known as having a bearish view. This is the scenario where a trader has a long put option.

Option Premium Prices

The pricing of options is not a one-size-fits-all scenario, and it can become rather complicated. There are pricing models that can help both sellers and buyers of options come up with a fair price and that list includes:

- **The Black-Scholes Model.** This is typically used to calculate European options.
- **The Binomial Option Pricing Model.** This is typically used to calculate American options.
- **Monte-Carlo Simulations.** Not only used in the finance industry, but this pricing option also calculates option premium by allowing the consideration for multiple outcomes, unlike the first two pricing models.

All of these models make calculations possible by factoring in certain stipulations. These conditions rely on factors that include:

- The value of the associated asset.
- The intrinsic value, which is the current value of the option and the potential increase that this option has over a specific amount of time. The intrinsic value is found by determining the difference in the current price of the associated asset and the strike price of the option.
- The time value, which is the extra amount that a trader is willing to pay if the option expires a few months away. It is the combination of intrinsic value and time value that make up the cost of an option premium.
- Volatility, which describes how likely that prices are to change on the financial market over a specific amount of time.

- Dividends, which are the distribution of fractions of a company's profit at a specific time period.
- Interest rates, which are a percentage charged for the use of money lent over a specific amount of time.

Trading Options Benefits

Trading options is a great investment opportunity because:

- The initial cost of getting started is lower than your typical investment opportunity involving the financial market.
- It costs less to invest in stock options compared to investing in buying stocks. This allows the trader to benefit from being in the same financial market as a stock's trader without actually paying for stocks upfront. This process is called hedging.
- Trader profit has the potential to be unlimited as it is linked to the rise and fall of the value of the associated asset.
- The trader or seller is not required to own the asset associated with the option to benefit from its value.
- The trader is under no obligation to actually buy or sell the asset associated with the contract unless this is beneficial to him or her.
- The strike price remains fixed throughout the length of the contract, so the trader does not have to worry about fluctuating prices.
- The options trader has great flexibility and several options. For example, there is the option to sell the same option to another investor or the option to exercise the right to buy or sell the asset.

- A trader can sell options on assets that he or she already owns to earn a passive income through premium payments.

Trading Options Disadvantages

As with anything that deals with finances, there are, of course, downsides to balance the advantages. The same is true of trading options. Some of the disadvantages of trading options include:

- Options are short-term investments with expiration dates that can be as short as one day long to only a few months long. This means that the trader needs to be on the ball with an exact strategy to profit from options. Options are typically not suited for an investor looking for long-term investments.
- There are additional costs associated with trading options apart from premium payments such as commissions to brokerage firms, etc.
- Trading options can expose the seller to unlimited losses because he or she is under contract to buy or sell the associated asset within a specific time frame if the trader decides to exercise the right to the option.
- An options trader needs to be qualified by a brokerage firm before he or she can begin to trade options.

As you can see, the benefits far exceed the disadvantages when it comes to trading options.

Chapter Summary

An option is a derivative financial contract that allows an investor to have the right to buy or sell the asset associated with the contract by an agreed-upon expiration date at a predetermined strike price. There are two main types of options, and they are called call options and put options. Call options allow the trader to exercise the right to buy the asset associated with that contract while put options allow the trader to exercise the right to sell the associated asset by the expiration date.

Options traders also have the choice of having a long position, which is described as the seller having ownership of the asset attached to the contract, or a short position, which is described as the position of the seller not having ownership of the asset attached to the contract.

Pricing options premiums can become a complicated affair and typically relies on a pricing model to be determined. Common pricing models include the Black-Scholes Model, The Binomial Option Pricing Model, and Monte-Carlo Simulations. These pricing models are typically based on factors such as the value of the asset, the intrinsic value of the option, the time value of the option, the volatility of the financial market, dividends and interest rates.

There are several advantages to trading options, and they include a relatively low initial investment, no obligation to buy or sell the associated asset, flexibility, the potential for unlimited profit for the trader, and the ability to earn passive income. Many traders choose to invest in options because these advantages outweigh the potential downsides of trading options, which include the short-term nature of such investments, having to become qualified to begin trading options, and the seller's exposure to unlimited losses.

Chapter 2: Day Trading Options Basics

There is more than one way to approach options trading. For example, there is the option to be a swing trader. A swing trader is one who takes on trading options as more of a part-time venture. On the other hand, if you want to really get in the thick of things, then being an options day trader is the right path for you.

What Options Day Traders Do

Unlike swing traders who bet on the asset value movement for months and investors who bet on the asset value movement for years, an options day trader bet on the movement of asset values for only one day. They open option positions at the beginning of the day and close them by the end of the day and repeat this the next day and the next.

This can seem like a sporadic action to an outside, uninformed looker, but the short-term nature of this action is what makes day trading so profitable for options traders who have mastered the right techniques and strategies. The risk of loss is reduced due to this fast turn of events because the efficient day trader will have a plan and a forecast for the result that will be obtained before opening a position at the start of the trading day.

The downside of this is that the day trader needs to ensure the positions that he or she opens will play out by the end of the trading day. The same factor of a short time that makes day trading options profitable can be a hindrance. This is why it is triply important that the day trader chooses the right options to pursue. This person needs to be efficient in these choices because having secure and reliable information is the options day trader's most powerful tool.

Options traders that partake in hedging do so to reduce the outright buying of the associated asset. They benefit from the activities on the financial market without putting down the kind of money that is needed to own the assets that are associated with particular financial activities. Trading options is just one of the financial activities that make use of the hedging process.

Options day traders do not hedge. They speculate. While hedgers are trying to protect themselves against asset price changes, the speculators are trying to profit from price changes. Options day traders are not trying to benefit from the future of the financial market. Rather, they are trying to benefit from current conditions on the financial market. So instead of trying to protect themselves from losses by managing their positions as hedgers do, they protect themselves with proper money management and the use of limit orders. A limit order is an instruction placed with the options day trader's bid to buy or sell the trader's position when the asset prices move in a certain direction.

How to Get Started As an Options Day Trader

Before you setup your options day trading business, there are a few things you need to have intimate knowledge of. They are your current financial circumstances, the time you are able to commit to day trading, and your risk profile. Create a financial balance sheet that lists your expenses and any other income that you obtain. This will allow you to assess your financial health and how much you can invest into options. This also allows you to know what risks you can take while trading options. Never invest capital or resources that you cannot afford to lose and never trade beyond your trading experience level. Becoming an options day trader requires a healthy time investment at the beginning because you need to learn your way around this arena as well as set up a strong foundation for your profile. Do not rush and squander your money in an overzealous move to get started.

Next, before you risk your hard-earned money, learn to trade options on paper. This is called Paper Trading and allows you to use real-life scenarios to assess your performance when it comes to trading options.

When you are ready to move forward to real-time practice, find a brokerage firm to represent you. Online brokerage firms are growing in popularity, but ensure that you properly research the firm to ensure reputability and that you are paying as little in commissions as possible. You may even be able to find a broker that does not charge commissions.

The brokerage firm will help you get set up as a qualified options trader at the level that is relevant for your experience as well as aid in setting up the appropriate accounts. You need to be able to process payments and other financial transfers online before you approach a broker.

Lastly, ensure that you have the tools for the trade. Ensure that your internet connection is fast and reliable. Also, ensure that your computer or laptop has a fast processor and adequate memory to prevent crashes as trading programs rely on a fast-moving computer. Most traders have a need for at least 2 monitors to keep abreast as to what is happing on the financial market.

Planning for Success

Options day trading is a business. You need to treat it as such. You will not wake up one day and just start any other type of business with no plan. Therefore, you need to approach day trading options with the same foresight and planning. Just as you would create a business plan for any other type of business, you need to create a trading plan. This will serve as your guide with step-by-step details on how you will approach day trading options, how you will measure your success, and how you will grow your business and income. As a result, here are a few vital categories that need to be developed in your trading plan:

Your Goals

Goal setting it a necessary life skill that everyone needs to learn, and it will serve you well in this area —these need to be both long-term and short-term. You need to be very specific. Vague notions like "I want to be as successful as I can be," have no place in your trading plan. Your goals need to be quantifiable and trackable.

Visualize where you want to be in the future and determined what needs to be done to make that mental picture a reality. Next, outline where you feel your career will be in the next 3 months, 6 months, 9 months, 1 year, 3 years, 5 years, and 10 years from today as you reach for that ultimate goal. As you are in this to succeed, you need to also outline the income that you would like to make and what you will do with the profits that you make.

Setting your goals also allows you to outline what areas you need to improve your knowledge so that you become a better options day trader. You need to develop a system for rewarding yourself when you hit milestones on your goal's list.

As an entrepreneur, you may find that your goals for your career overlap with your personal goals. This is no cause for concern because you are your business.

Entry Into the Options Trading Market

There are several different types of options that a day trader can pursue, but it makes no sense to try to pursue all of them as this will stretch you and your resources thin. The best thing to do is pinned down one or two niches that you will pursue at the beginning to find the ones that fit best with you and your trading style. Popular niches that day traders pursue include stocks, foreign exchange and exchange-traded funds.

An Efficient Workspace

You need to develop a plan for where you will work as well as the equipment that you will need. This does not have to be fancy. All you need is an adequate internet connection, a computer setup and a working filing system. Ensure that you have plans to upgrade your equipment as needed.

Developing a Time Schedule

Financial markets do not close even though many have set trading hours. Therefore, it is up to the options day trader to define his or her work hours. Some options day traders find it best to work in the early morning while others find it best to work late at night. The great thing about trading options is that it is a flexible career, and you can trade at almost any time of the day.

It is important to set regular trading hours to ensure that you do not become burnt out and that you maintain your perspective of your career and life. All work and no play leads to sickness. While you are setting working hours, also allocate time off, vacation and sick leave. Working yourself to the bone will remove the sense of fulfillment that you will find with this job. Therefore, finding balance is key.

Personal Development

As you are your business, you need to ensure that you invest in yourself so that you continuously expand your knowledge of trading and develop yourself as an individual. Schedule time for further reading, seminars, and other learning tools.

Your trading plan is not set in stone. In fact, it is something that you should continuously evaluate and revise based on the conditions and circumstances that you experience as an options day trader. At the very least, your options trading plan should be re-evaluated once yearly.

The Qualities of an Effective Options Day Trader

As mentioned earlier, it takes a special kind of person to be an effective and profitable options day trader. This is a fast-paced career and, as such, it cannot be done effectively if a person becomes undone easily by stress or has an inability to concentrate on the market and the figures in front of them. This figure needs to develop effective systems to help them keep on track and to make decisions that are not confounded by emotion. In essence, an options day trader needs to be able to keep a clear mind while still being analytical even under the most strenuous mental conditions.

As another pitch to help you know if options day trading is right for you, I have compiled a list of traits that an effective and efficient options day trader must have to be successful.

The first trait is being able to work well under pressure. Emotions can get to a trader in the form of fear, doubt and hope when it comes to trading options. Remember that decisions need to be made with a clear head, and these emotions need to be brushed aside because they are not relevant when it comes to opening option positions. The options trader needs to be able to unwind as well because keeping these emotions pent-up can lead to detrimental mental, emotional and physical health symptoms. This person needs to be able to find ways to get rid of this excess energy, and this can be in the form of initiating social contact with other persons outside of trading hours and engaging in physical activities such as yoga, meditation and exercise.

An effective options day trader is also a highly independent person because this person spends most of their time working by themselves. This is an age of technology and, so, day traders do not need to leave their house to be able to perform well in this career. In fact, options day trading can be performed from any part of the world as long as the options day trader has access to the internet and a computer. Some people cannot handle the isolation of this career and crack under pressure. An effective options day trader knows how to channel that energy so that he or she can be productive with the time alone, so that time with others can be more enjoyable and filled with quality.

An effective options day trader is an entrepreneur at heart. Being an options day trader means being your own boss. There will be no one hounding you to get things done on time. Therefore, if you cannot handle developing and maintaining an effective schedule to get work done, then this is not the career for you. As an options day trader, you need to be able to manage your time effectively so that you make the most profit in as little time as possible.

An effective day trader is also decisive. Remember that many things can happen in the space of a day. An options day trader cannot afford to be paralyzed by over-analysis. This person needs to be able to think quickly on their feet and make decisions just as fast because there is no luxury of waiting for tomorrow to make those decisions. An options day trader needs to be able to seize opportunities as soon as they come.

Chapter Summary

Unlike other types of options traders that assess value movement for months and, rarely, years, day traders bet on the movement of asset values for only one day. They open option positions at the beginning of the day and close them by the end of the day and repeat this the next day and the next.

Before you get started as an options day trader, you need to assess your current financial circumstances, the time you are able to commit to day trading and your risk profile. Also, practice paper trading before committing real money to trading options just so that you get the hang of it before you risk your hard-earned capital.

Ensure that you have a trading plan that outlines your goals, how you will start day trading options and a time schedule. An efficient options day trader also has an effective workspace that at least contains a computer with, a fast processor and memory, a fast, reliable internet connection, and a working filing system.

An options day trader has a few definitive traits to make this career lucrative and they include:

- Being able to work efficiently under pressure.
- Being independent.
- Being entrepreneurship-minded.
- Being decisive.

Chapter 3: The Trading Market

You need to know your way around the options market to leverage your daily investments. Many day traders begin with the stock market simply because there are many similar nuances between options and stocks. In fact, trading stocks is what most people immediately think of when they hear day trading. Therefore, it is in every option day trader to become familiar with the stock market as well, even though the trader should never confuse the two entities. This chapter is dedicated to gaining you information on the market influences that affect your success.

Deciding What Market to Trade-In

Before you jump into the market looking for options to trade, you need to decide what types of assets are good for day trading options. Not doing so will only leave you feeling dazed and confused because the market can seem endless. Yes, stocks are the easy, popular choice, but they are not the only choice, and they might not be the right choice for you. Futures, Forex, Cryptocurrencies and even Corn are also good options for day trading options. Stock trading is facilitated by the buying and selling of shares in a company's portfolio, and day trading stock options means that all positions must be opened by 9:30 AM EST and closed by 4 PM EST on the American stock market.

The future market is one where the contract is created between the seller and the trader to buy or sell a predetermined value of the associated asset at a future date. An options day trader can profit due to the price fluctuations that can happen in the space of a day. The day trader needs to be cautious with the futures market working hours because they can vary. As such, the trader needs to be aware of the time his or her position needs to close.

The forex market is accessible at any time of day and is the biggest financial market in the world. This market allows for the exchange of different currencies.

There are many more markets to choose from when starting your options day trading career, but it all boils down to your circumstances and the resources you have available to you. For example, startup fund can be an issue. This is particularly prevalent with the stock market. On the stock market, a trader needs to have an excess of $20,000 on his or her trading account to participate while the forex market allows trades that are as low as a few hundred dollars. Therefore, you can only pursue options in the stock and futures market if you have the capital to back you.

Time is another consideration. Remember that some markets like the stock market only function at certain times of the day, some fluctuate in time operation and others operate 24 hours a day.

The strategy is also a factor. We will speak on this in a later chapter, but some strategies work best in a certain market at certain times of day. Therefore, if there is a particular strategy that a day trader is great at, then he or she might have better results in certain markets.

How to Find the Best Options to Day Trade

After you have set your sights on a particular market, then you can move on to determine which particular assets you will pursue options in. You need to be able to pinpoint niches that work and luckily there are systems in place that can help you do that. Such tools include:

Technical Analysis

This is the first tool that we will discuss. It allows day traders to examine market sectors to identify strengths and weaknesses. By identifying those strengths and weaknesses, the options day trader can narrow down the options niches he or she would like to pursue within a given market.

There are several types of tools for performing technical analysis and they include:

- **Bollinger Band**, which is a measure of market volatility.
- **Intraday Momentum Index (IMI)**, which is an indicator of how options will play out within 1 day.
- **Open Interest (OI)**, which indicates the number of open options, contracts to determine trends in options.
- **Money Flow Index (MFI),** which indicates the flow of money into assets over a specific amount of time.
- **Relative Strength Index (RSI)**, which allows the trader to compare profits and losses over a set period of time.
- **Put-Call Ratio (PCR)**, which indicates the volume of the put options relative to call options.

Price Charts

These tools give a visual representation of price and volume information so that market trends can be determined. More precisely known as price charts because they show price movement over a specific amount of time, charts come in different types. Common types include:

Line Charts

These easy-to-interpret charts document price movement over a specific period of time, such as months or years. Each price data point is connected using a single line. While the biggest advantage this type of chart is the simplicity, this also causes a disadvantage to day traders as they provide no information about the strength of trading during the day.

The line chart also does not provide price gap information. A price gap is defined as the interval between one trading period that is completely above or below a previous trading period. This price cap information is critical for options day traders make effective decisions.

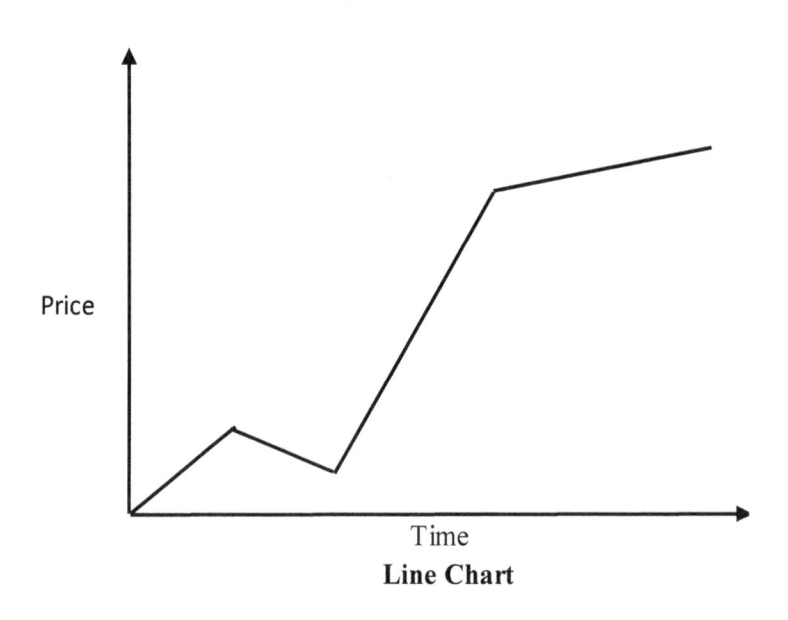

Line Chart

Open-High-Low-Close Bar Chart

This type of chart illustrates price movement from highest to lowest over as specific amounts of time, such as 1 hour or one day. It is so named because it shows open, high, low and close prices for the time period specified. The low to the high trading range is displayed with a vertical line while the opening and closing prices are displayed on a horizontal tab. All four elements make up one bar on the chart, and a series of these bars show movement over an extended period of time.

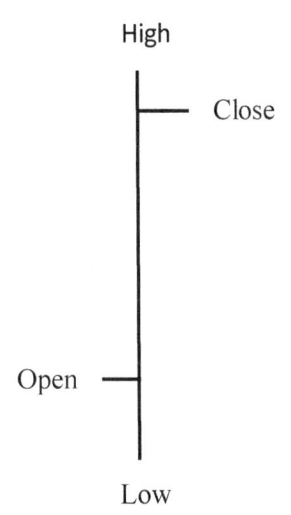

Example of Single Bar on Open-High-Low-Close Bar Chart

This type of bar chart is advantageous as an options day trading tool because it provides information over 1-day trading periods as well as price gap knowledge.

Candlestick Chart

This is the kind of chart that is used by professional options day traders. It is similar to the open-high-low-close bar chart and is represented by price on the vertical axis and time on the horizontal axis. As such, it depicts price movement over time.

43

The structure of the candlestick chart has individual components. They are called candlesticks, hence the name of the chart. Every candlestick has 3 parts. They are called:

- **The Body**: This depicts the open-to-close range.
- **The Wick:** This represents the daily highs and lows. It is also called the shadow.
- **The Color:** This depicts the direction of price movement. White or green indicates an upward price movement. Red or black indicates a price decline.

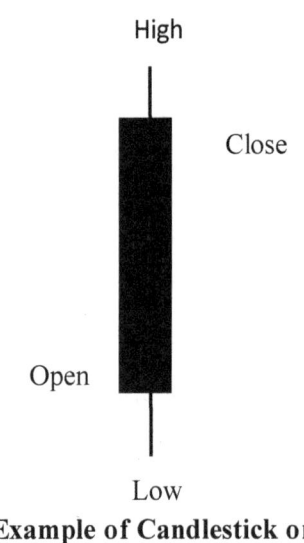

Example of Candlestick on Candlestick Chart

Using the candlestick chart allows day traders to see patterns on the market. There are several types of candlestick charts.

Factors That Affect the Options Market

After you have analyzed the options market and decided on the options that you will pursue, it is time to navigate the market and make a bet on the options you have decided on.

The first thing you need to do is execute a trade. If you are using an online broker as most options day traders do these days, you will make an order through the broker's digital system. When this is done, the options day trader needs to identify whether or not, he or she will be opening a new position or closing an existing position.

After this has successfully been executed, the trade details will be sent to the options day trader electronically.

Factors that affect how the option will play out include interest rates, economic trends and market volatility.

Chapter Summary

An options day trader needs to know his or her way around the options market to be effective at this career. The first thing the day trader needs to do is decide on the particular market that he or she will trade options in. The stock market is a popular choice, but it requires a high initial investment and has set hours for options trading.

The Futures and Forex Market are also popular options trading markets with different operating times and lower initial investment amount requirements. These might work better for some options day traders.

After the options day trader has figured out the particular market that he or she will trade options in, he or she has to pick a particular niche within that market to trade options in. Using technical analysis and price charts like the line chart, open-high-low-close bar chart, and candlestick chart help options day traders decide on the best options to pursue.

After this decision has been made, the day trader will execute the options trade via the brokerage firm he or she works with. This is typically done online as most options day traders turn to digital means in this age of technology. The success of how this options trade will play out is affected by factors like interest rates, economic trends and market volatility.

Chapter 4: Options Day Trading Styles

No matter what style or strategy an options day trader chooses to use, he or she needs to factor in three important components every single time. These elements are:

- **Liquidity**: This factor describes how quickly an option or other asset can be bought and sold without the current market price being affected. Liquid options are more desirable to an options day trader because they trade easier. Illiquid options create more resistance in the ease at which a trader can open or close his or her position. This extends the time needed to complete the transactions involved and thus can lead to a loss for the options day trader.
- **Volatility:** This describes how sensitive the assets attached to the options, is to price changes due to external factors. Some assets are more volatile than others. Stocks and Cryptocurrencies are volatile assets.

Volatility has a great impact on an options day trader's profit margin.

- **Volume:** This describes the number of options being traded at a specific time interval. Volume is an indication of the associated asset price movement on the market because it is a gage of the asset's interest in the market. The higher the volume, the more desirable traders typically are in pursuing an option. Volume is one of the factors that make up open interest, which is the total number of active options. Active options have not been liquidated, exercised or assigned. If an options trader ignores taking action on options for too long, this can make circumstances unfavorable, which can lead to unnecessary losses. An options trader needs to always be on the ball about closing options positions at the appropriate time.

To take advantage of the options day trading choices listed below, the day trader needs to be very familiar with these factors and how he or she can use them to his or her advantage.

Breakout Options Day Trading

Breakout describes the process of entering the market when prices move out of their typical price range. For this style of trading to be successful, there needs to be an accompanying increase in volume. There is more than one type of breakout, but we will discuss one of the most popular, which is called support and resistance breakouts.

The support and resistance method describes the point at which the associated asset price stops decreasing (support) and the point at which the associated asset price stops increasing (resistance). The day trader will enter a long position if the associated asset price breaks above resistance. On the other hand, the options day trader will enter a short position if the associated asset breaks below the supported price. As you can see, the position that the trader takes depends on if the asset is supported or resisted at that new price level. As the asset transcends the normal price barrier, volatility typically increases. This usually results in the price of the associated asset moving in the direction of the breakout.

When contemplating this trading style, the options day trader needs to carefully deliberate his or her entry points and exit strategies. The typical entry strategy depends on whether or not the prices are set to close above the resistance level or below the support level. The day trader will take on a bearish position if this price is said to be above the resistance level. A bullish approach is a typical maneuver if prices are set to close below the support.

Exit strategies require a more sophisticated approach. The options day trader needs to consider past performance and use chart patterns to determine a price target to close his or her position. Once the target has been reached, the day trader can exit the trade and enjoy the profit earned.

Momentum Options Day Trading

This options day trading style describes the process of options day trading relying on price volatility and the rate of change of volume. It is so-called because the main idea behind the strategy is that the force behind the price movement of the associated asset is enough to sustain it in the same direction. This is because when an asset increases in price, it typically attracts investors, which drives the price even higher. Options day traders who use this style ride that momentum and make a profit off the expected price movement.

This style is based on using technical analysis to track the price movement of the associated asset. This analysis gives the day trader an overall picture that includes momentum indicators like:

- **The Momentum Indicator,** which makes use of the most recent closing price of the associated asset to determine the strength of the price movement as a trend.
- **The Relative Strength Index (RSI)**, which is a comparison of profits and losses over a set period of time.
- **Moving Averages**, which allows the day trader to see passed fluctuations to analyze the trends in the market.

- **The Stochastic Oscillator**, which is a comparison of the most recent closing prices of the associated asset over a specified period of time.

Momentum options day trading is highly effective and simple as long as it is done right. The day trader needs to keep abreast of the news and earnings reports to make informed decisions using this trading style.

Reversal Options Day Trading

This style relies on trading against the trend and is, in essence, the opposite of momentum options day trading. Also called trend trading or pull back trending, it is performed when an options day trader is able to identify pullbacks against the current price movement trends. Clearly, this is a risky move, but it can be quite profitable when the trade goes according to plan. Because of the depth of market knowledge and trading experience that is needed to perform this style effectively, it is not one that is recommended for beginners to practice.

This is a bullish approach to options trading and entails buying an out of the money call option as well as selling an out of the money put option. Both profit and loss are potentially unlimited.

Scalping Options Day Trading

This options day trading style refers to the process of buying and selling the same associated asset several times in the same day. This is profitable when there is extreme volatility on the market. The options day trader makes his profit by buying an options position at a lower price, then selling it for a higher price or selling an options position at a higher price and buying it at a lower price depending on whether or not this is a call or a put option.

This style of options trading is extremely reliant on liquidity. Illiquid options should not be used with this style because the options day trader needs to be able to open and close these types of trades several times during the space of one day. Trading liquid options allow the day trader to gain maximum profitability when entering and to exit trades.

The typical strategy is to trade several small options during the course of the day to accumulate profit rather than trying to trade big infrequently. Trading big with this particular style can lead to huge losses in the space of only a few hours. This is why this style is only recommended for disciplined options day traders who are content with seeking small, repeated profits even though it is a less risky method compared to the others.

Due to the nature of this style, it is the shortest form of options day trading because it does not even last the whole day – only a few hours. Day traders who practice this style are known as scalpers. Technical analysis is required to assess the best bets with the price movement of the associated assets.

Scalping is an umbrella term that encompasses several different methods of scalping. There is time and sales scalping, whereby the day trader uses passed records of bought, sold and cancelled transactions to determine the best options to trade and when the best times for these transactions are. Other types of scalping involve the use of bars and charts for analysis of the way forward.

Using Pivot Points for Options Day Trading

This options day trading style is particularly useful in the Forex Market. It describes the act of pivoting or reserving after a support or resistance level has been reached at the market price. It works in much the same way that it does with support and resistance breakouts.

The typical strategies with this particular options day trading style are:

- To buy the position if the support level is being approached, then placing a stop just below that level.
- To sell the position if the resistance level is being approached, then placing a stop just below that level.

To determine the point of the pivot, the day trader will analyze the highs and lows of the previous day's trading and the closing prices of the previous day. This is calculated with this formula:

(High + Low + Close)/3=Pivot Point

Using the pivot point, the support and resistance levels can be calculated as well. The formulas for the first support and resistance levels are as follows:

(2 x Pivot Point)−High=First Support Level

(2 x Pivot Point)−Low= First Resistance Level

The second support and resistance levels are calculated with the following formulas:

Pivot Point−(First Resistance Level − First Support Level) = Second Support Level

Pivot Point+ (First Resistance Level − First Support Level) = Second Resistance Level

The options trading range that is most profitable lies when the pivot point is between the first support and resistance levels.

The options day trader is vulnerable to sudden price movements with his style of trading. This can result in serious losses if it is not managed. To limit losses with this strategy, the options day trader can implement stops to marginalize losses. This is typically placed just above the recent high price close when the day trader has taken on a short position. This is placed just below a recent low when the day trader had taken on a long position. To be doubly safe, the options day trader can also place two stops, such as placing a physical stop at the most capital that he or she can afford to part with and another where an exit strategy is implemented.

Where these stops are placed is also dependent on volatility.

Chapter Summary

No matter what style or strategy an options day trader chooses to use, he or she needs to factor in three important components every single time. These elements are:

- **Liquidity**, which describes how quickly an option or other asset can be bought and sold without the current market price being affected.
- **Volatility**, which describes how sensitive the asset attached to the options, is to price changes due to external factors.
- **Volume**, which describes the number of options being traded at a specific time interval.

The different types of options day trading styles include:

- **Breakout Options Day Trading**, which describes the process of entering the market when prices move out of their typical price range. There is more than one type of breakout. One of the most popular methods of breaking out is called support and resistance breakouts. The support and resistance method describes the point at which the associated asset price stops decreasing (support) and the point at which the associated asset price stops increasing (resistance).
- **Momentum Options Day Trading**, which describes the process of day trading relying on price volatility and

the rate of change of volume. It is so-called because the price movement of the associated asset is enough to sustain it in the same direction. This is because when an asset increases in price, it typically attracts investors, which drives the price even higher. This style is based on using technical analysis to track the momentum indicators like momentum indicator, the Relative Strength Index (RSI), moving averages, and the stochastic oscillator.

- **Reversal Options Day Trading**, which relies on trading against the trend. It is performed when a day options trader is able to identify pullbacks against the current price movement trends. This style is only suitable for advanced options day traders.
- **Scalping Options Day Trading**, which is the process of buying and selling the same associated asset several times in the same day. This is profitable when there is extreme volatility on the market. The options day trader makes his profit by buying an options position at a lower price, then selling it for a higher price or selling an options position at a higher price and buying it at a lower price depending on whether or not this is a call or a put option. This style of options trading is extremely reliant on liquidity.
- **Using Pivot Points for Options Day Trading**, which describes the act of pivoting or reserving after a support or resistance level has been reached at the market

price. This options day trading style is particularly useful in the forex market and works in much the same way that it does with support and resistance breakouts.

These options day trading styles can be mixed and matched so that a day trader knows the ones that work best for him or her and in what combination.

Chapter 5: Trading Options Strategies Every Day Trader Should Know

There are plenty of options trading strategies to choose from. Some are suitable for beginners, while others should only be practiced by advanced options traders who know the market well and have the experience to back them. Even if a beginner is advised not to practice a particular strategy at that point in his or her career, being aware that the strategy exists is useful as this allows the trader to be aware of alternatives as well as gives this person strategies to work toward to make their daily trading more efficient and profitable.

The strategies listed below and expanded into an overview have been placed in alphabetical order for easy reference.

Covered Call Strategy

This strategy is also known as a buy-write because it relays the fact that this is a two-part process whereby the trader first buys the associated asset then sells the right to purchase that asset via an option. Stock is the most common associated asset with this strategy. The trader lowers the risk to himself or herself because he or she owns the asset and receives a premium payment from the holder of the contract. While the asset may still be in the owner's possession after the contract has expired if the trader decides not to exercise the right, the owner needs to be willing to part with the asset if the trader does indeed decide to exercise that right.

The profit earned by the seller is achieved if the asset price meets or goes above the strike price on or by the expiration date. This is calculated with this formula:

Premium+ (Strike Price - Asset Price) = Potential Profit

This profit is limited.

Breakeven is calculated like this:

Purchase Price of the Asset - Premium = Breakeven

This strategy appeals to many investors because there is guaranteed payment of the option premium whether or not the option holder decides to exercise the right to the option. The seller can set up a regular income stream in markets that are bullish or comparatively neutral. There is also the benefit of the seller being covered from risk due to ownership of the asset.

The risks include the seller losing due to the asset price potentially decreasing below the breakeven point and potentially experiencing an opportunity cost if the price of the asset skyrockets.

Credit Spreads

This strategy describes the selling of a high-premium option while purchasing a low-premium option type, which is a call or put, in an effort to make a profit when the spread between the two options narrows. The options will have the same expiration date but different strike prices, hence the potential for profit.

The appeal of credit spreads is that they have lowered risk if the price movement goes against the trader, making losses limited—the seller benefits from the premium payment.

The disadvantage is that profits are limited, just like losses.

There are different types of credit spreads. They include:

- **Bear Call Spread**, which is a beginner-friendly strategy. It employs a bearish outlook that relies on the price of the associated asset decreasing modestly. The trader buys 1 out of the money call option and sells 1 in the money put option. Profit is gained by finding the difference between the option premium and the commissions paid. The loss occurs when the asset price increases below the strike price.
- **Bull Put Spread**, which is a beginner-friendly strategy with a bearish outlook that relies on the price of the associated asset decreasing substantially. The trader buys 1 out of the money put option of a higher premium and sells 1 on the money put option of a lower premium.

Profit is gained by finding the difference between the option premium and the commissions paid. The loss occurs when the asset price decreases below the strike price.

- **Iron Butterfly Spread,** which involves 4 transactions. The options trader is buying 1 out of the money call option, selling 1 at the money call option, buying 1 out of the money put option and selling 1 at the money put option, all with the same expiration date and associated asset. This is a complex strategy that is not recommended for beginners.
- **Short Butter Spread,** which entails 3 transactions. The transactions are buying 1 out of the money call/put option, selling 1 out of the money call/put option and buying 1 at the money call/put option. They all have the same expiration date and associated asset. This is also a complex strategy that is not recommended for beginners.

Debit Spreads.

This strategy describes the buying of a high-premium option while purchasing a low-premium option type in an effort to make a profit when the spread between the two options widen. Just like with credit spreads, the options will have the same expiration date but different strike prices, which leaves the potential for profit.

The benefits of Debit Spreads include limited losses and being able to better predict losses and profits. The disadvantage is that profits are limited.

There are different types of debit spreads as well. They include:

- **Bear Put Spread**, which is a bearish strategy that requires 2 transactions, which are the buying of 1 at the money put option and the selling of 1 on the money put option. This is done because the trader is betting that the price movement of the associated asset will go down. Profit is earned when the price of the associated asset is the same as the strike price of the put option.
- **Bull Call Spread,** which is a bullish strategy that includes 2 transactions, which are the buying of 1 at the money call option and the selling of 1 out of the money call option. A trader implements this strategy when he or she thinks that the price movement of the associated asset will go up modestly. Profit is gained when the price of the associated asset is the same at the strike price of the short call option.
- **Butterfly Spread**, which is a neutral strategy that involves 3 transactions whereby the trader buys 1 in the money call option, sells 2 at the money call option and buys 1 on the money call option. Both profits and losses are limited to this type of spread strategy. Profit is

gained when the price of the associated asset remained the same on the date of expiration.
- **Reverse Iron Butterfly**, which is a volatile strategy that involves 4 transactions. These transactions are the selling of 1 out at the money put option, buying 1 at the money put option, buying 1 at the money call option and selling 1 out of the money call option. Profit is gained when the price of the associated asset falls.

Iron Condor

This is a neutral strategy that is best practiced by advanced options traders because of its complex nature. It is comprised of 4 transactions. They are:

- Selling 1 out of the money put option.
- Buying 1 out of the money put option (has the lower strike).
- Selling 1 out of the money call option.
- Buying 1 out of the money call option (has the highest strike).

All of these transactions have the same expiration date and are attached to the same associated asset. Profit is gained when the price of the associated asset is between the call and put options that are sold. Loss is limited just as profit is with this strategy.

Many traders use this strategy because the asset price can go in any direction and the trader can still make a profit; it is flexible and potential losses and profits can be predetermined.

This strategy has 4 transactions, and as such the complexity can be off-putting to some traders.

Rolling Out Options

This strategy involves closing one option, then replacing it with an identical option to manage a winning or losing position. This management comes in the form of the newly opened position having the same associated asset but varied terms. These terms are typically the adjustment of the strike price and how long the trader would like to hold a long or short position.

Rolling can be done in 3 ways. They are:

- **Rolling Up**, which is the process of closing an existing option position and simultaneously opening a similar position with a higher strike price.
- **Rolling Down**, which is the process of closing an existing option position and simultaneously opening a similar position with a lower strike price.
- **Rolling Forward**, which is the process of moving an open position to a different expiration date so that the length of the contract is extended.

This strategy is easy enough to be practiced by beginners.

Straddle Strategy

This strategy is employed so that the options trader protects himself or herself from loss, whether the asset price moves up or down. There are short straddles and long straddles.

The short straddle is also called a sell straddle or a naked straddle. It is a neutral strategy that entails the trader selling 1 at the money call option and 1 at the money put option with the same expiration date, same strike price, and having the same associated asset. Profit from this strategy is limited and is calculated by finding the difference between the options premium and commissions paid.

The loss has the potential to be unlimited if the asset price moves sharply up or down.

The Long Straddle is also called a Buy Straddle. It is a neutral strategy and involves the trader buying 1 at the money call option and 1 at the money put option with the same expiration date, strike price, and associated asset.

The profit potential is unlimited, and the risk of loss is limited.

Strangle Strategy

This is a strategy that is used when a trader bets that an asset price will move up or down, but still gathers protection in the event that he or she is wrong. Strangles come in both a long and short variety.

The long strangle is also called a buy strangle, and it is a neutral options trading strategy. This strategy entails the trader buying 1 out of the money put option and 1 out of the money call option. This is done because the trader expects volatility on the market. Profit is potentially unlimited and happens if the asset price moves sharply up or down. Loss is limited and is the combination of the options premium and the commission paid.

The Short Strangle is also called a Sell Strangle. It is used as a neutral trading strategy, and so the trader sells 1 out of the money put option and 1 out of the money call option. Both of these options have the same expiration date and the same asset associated. This is a short-term strategy used when the trader expects the asset price to remain relatively stable on the market. Profit is limited and is the difference between the option premium and commissions paid for that option. Risk is unlimited. Loss can be experienced if the price of the asset goes up or down sharply.

Chapter Summary

There are a lot of options trading strategies to choose from. There are strategies that are appropriate for all levels of day options trading, including beginner, intermediate and advanced. Some of these strategies include:

- **Covered Call Strategy**, which is a two-part process whereby the trader first buys the associated asset, then sells the right to purchase that asset via an option.
- **Credit Spreads**, which describes the selling of a high-premium option while purchasing a low-premium option to make a profit when the spread between the two options narrows.
- **Debit Spreads**, which describes the buying of a high-premium option while purchasing a low-premium option type to make a profit when the spread between the two options widen.
- **Iron Condor**, which is a neutral strategy that is best practiced by advanced options traders because of its complex nature. It is comprised of 4 transactions.
- **Rolling Out Options**, which is the strategy that involves closing one option then replacing it with an identical option to manage a winning or losing position so that varied terms are applied to the same associated asset.
- **Straddle Strategy**, which is employed so that the options trader protects himself or herself from loss, whether the asset price moves up or down. The short straddle is a neutral strategy that entails the trader selling 1 at the money call option and 1 at the money put option with the same expiration date, same strike price, and having the same associated asset. The long straddle is a neutral strategy that involves the trader

buying 1 at the money call option and 1 at the money put option with the same expiration date, strike price and associated asset.

- **Strangle Strategy**, which is used when a trader bets that an asset price will move up or down but still gathers protection in the event that he or she is wrong. The long strangle entails the trader buying 1 out of the money put option and 1 out of the money call option while the short strangle entails the trader selling 1 out of the money put option and 1 out of the money call option.

Chapter 6: Power Principles to Ensure a Strong Entry Into Day Trading Options

I cannot stress this enough - you need to have a plan if you want to be successful at day trading options. You are putting your money on the line every day. I am sure squandering those hard-earned funds is not the plan, but that is exactly what will happen without a proper plan in place. Obviously, having a trading plan in place is a given as we discussed earlier, but that plan is not enough. You need to take it a step further by applying principles that will reinforce that plan. Think of that trading plan as the foundation of your house of success. The principles that we will discuss below are the bricks to develop your house into what you want it to be.

Power Principle #1 – Ensure Good Money Management

Money is the tool that keeps the engine of the financial industry performing in good working order. It is essential that you learn to manage your money in a way that works for you instead of against you as an options day trader. It is an intricate part of managing your risk and increasing your profit.

Money management is the process whereby monies are allocated for spending, budgeting, saving, investing and other processes. Money management is a term that any person with a career in the financial industry, and particularly in the options trading industry, is intimately familiar with because this allocation of funds is the difference between a winning options trader and a struggling options trader.

Below you will find tips for managing your money so that you have maximum control of your options day trading career.

Money Management Tips for Options Traders

- Define money goals for the short term and the long term, so that you can envision what you would like to save, invest, etc. Ensure that these are recorded and easily accessed. Your trading plan will help you define your money goals.
- Develop an accounting system. There are wide ranges of software that can help with this, but it does not matter which one you use as long as you are able to establish records and easily track the flow of your money.
- Use the position sizing to manage your money. Position sizing is the process of determining how much money

will be allocated to entering an options position. To do this effectively, allocated a smart percentage of your investment funds toward individual options. For example, it would be unwise to use 50% of your investment fund on one option. That is 50% of your capital that can potentially go down the drain if you make a loss in that position. A good percentage is using no more than 10% of your investment fund toward individual option positions. This percentage allocation will help you get through tough periods, which eventually happen without having all your funds being lost.

- NEVER, ever invest money that you cannot afford to lose. Do not let emotion override this principle and cloud your judgment.
- Spread your risks by diversifying your portfolio. You diversify your portfolio by spreading your wealth by investing in different areas; add to your investments regularly, being aware of commissions at all times, and knowing when to close a position.
- Develop the day trading styles and strategies that earn you a steady rate of return. Even if you use scalping where the returns are comparatively small, that steady flow of profit can add up big over time.

Power Principle #2 – Ensure That Risks and Rewards Are Balanced

To ensure that losses are kept to a minimum and that returns are as great as they can be, options day traders should use the risk/reward ratio to determine each and to make adjustments as necessary. The risk/reward ratio is an assessment used to show the profit potential in relation to potential losses. This requires knowing the potential risks and profits associated with an options trade. Potential risks are managed by using a stop-loss order. A stop-loss order is a command that allows you to exit a position in an options trade once a certain price threshold has been reached.

Profit is targeted using an established plan. The potential profit is calculated by finding the difference between the entry price and the target profit. This is calculated by dividing the expected return on the options investment by the standard deviation.

Another way to manage risks and rewards is by diversifying your portfolio. Always spread your money across different assets, financial sectors and geographies. Ensure that these different facets of your portfolio are not closely related to each other so that if one goes down, they do not all fall. Be smart about protecting and building your wealth.

Power Principle #3 – Develop a Consistent Monthly Options Trading System

The aim of doing options trading daily is to have an overall winning options trading month. That will not happen if you trade options here and there. You cannot expect to see a huge profit at the end of the month if you only performed 2 or 3 transactions.

You need to have a high options trading frequency to up the chances of coming out winning every month. The only way to do that is to develop a system where you perform options trades at least 5 days a week.

To have consistently good months, you need to develop strong daily systems that keep your overall monthly average high. Therefore, creating a daily options trading schedule is key. Here is an example of an efficient options day trading schedule:

1. **Perform market analysis.** This needs to be done before the markets open in the morning. That means that the options day trader needs to get an early start on the day. This entails checking the news to scan for any major events that might affect the markets that day, checking the economic calendar; and assessing the actions of other day traders to assess volume and competition.

2. **Manage your portfolio.** The way that an options day trader does this is dependent on the strategies that he or she implements, but overall, it is about assessing positions that you already have or are contemplating for efficient management of entry and exits that day. It also allows for good money management.
3. **Enter new positions.** After assessing the market and fine-tuning your portfolio, the next step is to enter new trades that day. Research and efficient decision-making go into this step. The options trader who has already determined how the market was doing and forecasted for performance that day would have noticed relevant patterns. The key here is to enter trades frequently via a sound strategy. To narrow done which positions you would like to pursue, keep an eye on the bullish, bearish, neutral and volatile watch lists, and run technical scans.

4. **Incorporate learning during the day.** Continual learning is something that an options trader needs to pursue, but this does not always have to be in the way of formal classes or courses. You can up your knowledge of options and day trading by following mentors, reading books, listening to podcasts, reading blogs, and watching videos online. Such activities are easy to incorporate into your daily routine. Even just a few minutes of study a day can go considerably up your

options day trading game in addition to stimulating your mind. Being in regular contact with other options day traders is also a great way of increasing your information well.

Power Principle #4 – Consider a Brokerage Firm That is Right for Your Level of Options Expertise

We touched briefly on brokerage firms in the beginning chapters of this book, but I want to again stress how important this decision is on an options day trader's profit margin. There are four important factors that you need to consider when choosing a broker and they are:

- The requirements for opening a cash and margin account.
- The unique services and features that the broker offers.
- The commission fees and other fees charged by the broker.
- The reputation and level of options expertise of the broker.

Let's take a look at these individual components to see how you can use them to power up your options day trading experience.

Broker Cash and Margin Accounts

Every options trader needs to open a cash account and margin account to be able to perform transactions. They are simply tools of the trade. A cash account is one that allows an options day trader to perform transactions via being loaded with cash. Margin accounts facilitates transactions by allowing that to borrow money against the value of security in his or her account. Both of these types of accounts require that a minimum amount be deposited. This can be as few as a few thousand dollars to tens of thousands of dollars, depending on the broker of choice. You need to be aware of the requirements when deliberating, which brokerage firm is right for you.

Broker Services and Features

There are different types of services and features available from different brokerage firms. For example, if an options trader would like to have an individual broker assigned to him or her to handle his or her own account personally, then he or she will have to look for a full-service broker. In this instance, there minimum account requirements that need to be met. Also, commission fees and other fees are generally higher with these types of brokerage firms. While the fees are higher, this might be better for a beginner trader to have that full service dedicated to their needs and the learning curve.

On the other hand, if an options trader does not have the capital needed to meet the minimum requirements of a full-service broker or would prefer to be more in charge of his or her own option trades, then there is the choice of going with a discount brokerage firm. The advantage to discount brokerage firms is that they tend to have lower commissions and fees. Most internet brokerage firms are discount brokers.

Other features that you need to consider when choosing a brokerage firm include:

- Whether or not the broker streams real-time quotes.
- The speed of execution for claims.
- The availability of bank wire services.
- The availability of monthly statements.
- How confirmations are done, whether written or electronic.

Commissions and Other Fees

Commission fees are paid when an options trader enters and exits positions. Every brokerage firm has its own commission fees set up. These are typically developed around the level of account activity and account size of the options trader.

These are not the only fees that an option trader needs to consider when considering brokerage firms. Many brokerage firms charge penalty fees for withdrawing funds and not maintaining minimum account balances—obviously, the existence of fees such as these cuts on an options trader's profit margin. The payment of fees needs to be kept to a minimum to gain maximum income and as such, an options trader needs to be aware of all fees that exist and how they are applied when operating with a brokerage firm. This needs to be done before signing up.

Broker Reputation and Options Expertise

You do not want to be scammed out of your money because you chose the wrong brokerage firm. Therefore, it is important that you choose a broker that has an established and long-standing reputation for trading options. You also want to deal with a brokerage firm that has great customer service, that can aid in laying the groundwork for negotiating reduced commissions and allows for flexibility. Options trading is a complex service and your brokerage firm needs to be able to provide support when you are handling difficult transactions.

A list of reputable online brokerage firms include:

- E*Trade.
- OptionsXpress.
- Scottrade.
- Ameritrade.
- Train Station.

You can look up any of these brokerage websites and find that they have a long-standing reputation for quality service. Even though most are based in the United States, many accept international accounts.

Power Principle #5 – Ensure That Exits Are automated

Even though I have stated that emotions should be set aside when trading options, we are all human and emotions are bound to come into the equation at some point. Knowing this, it is imperative that systems be developed to minimize the impact of emotions. Having your exits automated is one such step that you can take to ensure that emotions are left out when dealing with options day trading. Using bracket orders facilitates this.

A bracket order is an instruction given when an options trader enters a new position that specifies a target or exit and stop-loss order that aligns with that. This order ensures that a system is set up to record two points – the target for-profit and the maximum loss point that will be tolerated before the stop-loss comes into effect. The execution of either order cancels the other.

Chapter Summary

Strength your options day trading plan and strategies with these power principles:

- Ensure good money management.
- Ensure that risks and rewards are balanced.
- Develop a consistent monthly options trading system.

- Consider a brokerage firm that is right for your level of options expertise.
- Ensure that exits are automated.

Chapter 7: 11 Options Day Trading Rules for Success

There is more to options day trading to just having a style or a strategy. If that was all it took, then you could just adopt those that are proven to work and just stick with them. Yes, options day trading styles and strategy are important, but they are not the end-all-be-all of this career.

The winning factor is the options day trader himself or herself. *You* are the factor that determines whether or not you will win or lose in this career —only taking the time to develop your expertise, seeking guidance when necessary and being totally dedicated allows a person to move from a novice options day trader to an experienced one that is successful and hitting his or her target goals.

To develop into the options day trader you want to be, being disciplined is necessary. There are options day trading rules that can help you develop that necessary discipline. You will make mistakes. Every beginner in any niche does and even experienced options day traders are human and thus, have bad days too.

Knowing common mistakes helps you avoid many of these mistakes and takes away much of the guesswork. Having rules to abide by helps you avoid these mistakes as well.

Below, I have listed 11 rules that every options day trader must know. Following them is entirely up to you, but know that they are proven to help beginner options day trader turn into winning options day traders.

The Rule for Success #1 – Have Realistic Expectations

It is sad to say that many people who enter the options trading industry are doing so to make a quick buck. Options trading is not a get-rich-quick scheme. It is a reputable career that has made many people rich, but that is only because these people have put in the time, effort, study and dedication to learning the craft and mastering it. Mastery does not happen overnight, and beginner options day traders need to be prepared for that learning curve and to have the fortitude to stick with day trading options even when it becomes tough.

Losses are also part of the game. No trading style or strategy will guarantee gains all the time. In fact, the best options traders have a winning percentage of about 80% and a losing average of approximately 20%. That is why an options day trader needs to be a good money manager and a good risk manager. Be prepared for eventual losses and be prepared to minimize those losses.

The Rule for Success #2 – Start Small to Grow a Big Portfolio

Caution is the name of the game when you just get started with day trading options. Remember that you are still learning options trading and developing an understanding of the financial market. Do not jump the gun even if you are eager. After you have practiced paper trading, start with smaller options positions, and steadily grow your standing as you get a lay of the options day trading land. This strategy allows you to keep your losses to a minimum and to develop a systematic way of entering positions.

The Rule for Success #3 – Know Your Limits

You may be tempted to trade as much as possible to develop a winning monthly average, but that strategy will have the opposite effect and land you with a losing average. Remember that every options trader needs careful consideration before that contract is set up. Never overtrade and tie up your investment fund.

The Rule for Success #4 – Be Mentally, Physically and Emotionally Prepared Every Day

This is a mentally, physically and emotionally tasking career, and you need to be able to meet the demands of this career. That means keeping your body, mind and heart in good health at all times. Ensure that you schedule time for self-care every day. That can be as simple as taking the time to read for recreation to having elaborate self-care routine carved out in the evenings.

Not keeping your mind, heart and head in optimum health mean that they are more likely to fail you. Signs that you need to buckle up and care for yourself more diligently include being constantly tired, being short-tempered, feeling preoccupied, and being easily distracted.

To ensure you perform your best every day, here a few tasks that you need to perform:

- Get the recommended amount of sleep daily. This is between 7 and 9 hours for an adult.
- Practice a balanced diet. The brain and body need adequate nutrition to work their best. Include fruits, complex carbs, and veggies in this diet and reduce the consumption of processed foods.
- Eat breakfast, lunch and dinner every day. Fuel your mind and body with the main meals. Eating a healthy

breakfast is especially important because it helps set the tone for the rest of the day.
- Exercise regularly. Being inactive increases your risk of developing chronic diseases like heart disease, certain cancers, and other terrible health consequences. Adding just a few minutes of exercise to your daily routine not only reduces those risks, but also allows your brain to function better, which is a huge advantage for an options day trader.
- Drink alcohol in moderation or not at all.
- Stop smoking.
- Reduce stress contributors in your environment.

The Rule for Success #5 – Do Your Homework Daily

Get up early and study the financial environment before the market opens and look at the news. This allows you to develop a daily options trading plan. The process of analyzing the financial climate before the market opens is called pre-market preparation. It is a necessary task that needs to be performed every day to asset competition and to align your overall strategy with the short-term conditions of that day.

An easy way to do this is to develop a pre-market checklist. An example of a pre-market checklist includes, but is not limited to:

- Checking the individual markets that you frequently trade options in or plan to trade options in to evaluate support and resistance.
- Checking the news to assess whether events that could affect the market developed overnight.
- Assessing what other options traders are doing to determined volume and competition.
- Determining what safe exits for losing positions are.
- Considering the seasonality of certain markets are some as affected by the day of the week, the month of the year, etc.

The Rule for Success #6 – Analyze Your Daily Performance

To determine if the options day trading style and strategies that you have adopted are working for you, you need to track your performance. At the most basic, this needs to be done on a daily basis by virtue of the fact that you are trading options daily. This will allow you to notice patterns in your profit and loss. This can lead to you determining the why and how of these gains and losses. These determinations lead to fine-tuning your daily processes for maximum returns. These daily performance reviews allow you to also make determinations on the long-term activity of your options day trading career.

The Rule for Success #7 – Do Not Be Greedy

If you are fortunate enough to make a 100% return on your investment, do not be greedy and try to reap more benefit from the position. You might have the position turn on you, and you can lose everything. When and if such a rare circumstance happens to you, sell your position and take the profits.

The Rule for Success #8 – Pay Attention to Volatility

Volatility speaks to how likely a price change will occur over a specific amount of time on the financial market. Volatility can work for an options day trader or against the options day trader. It all depends on what the options day trader is trying to accomplish and what his or her current position is.

There are many external factors that affect volatility and such factors include the economic climate, global events and news reports. Strangles and straddles strategies are great for use in volatile markets.

There are different types of volatility and they include:

- **Price Volatility**, which describes how the price of an asset increases or decreases based on the supply and demand of that asset.
- **Historical Volatility**, which is a measure of how an asset has performed over the last 12 months.

- **Implied Volatility**, which is a measure of how an asset will perform in the future.

The Rule for Success #9 – Use the Greeks

The Greeks are a collection of measures that provide a gage of an option's price sensitivity in relation to other factors. Each Greek is represented by a letter from the Greek alphabet. These Greeks use complex formulas to be determined, but they are the system that option pricing is based on. Even though these calculations can be complex, they can be done quickly and efficiently so that options day traders can use them as a method of advancing their trades for the most profitable position.

The 5 Greeks that are used in options trading are:

Delta

This Greek defines the price relationship between an option and its associated asset. Delta is a direct translation of a change in the price of the associated asset into the changing of the price of an option. Call options deltas to range from 1 to 0 while put options deltas range from 0 to -1. An example of delta as it relates to a call option is a call option with a delta of 0.5. If the price of the associated asset increases by $200, then the price of the call option will increase by $100.

Vega

This Greek is a measure of the sensitivity of the price of an option to the implied volatility of the associated asset. Option prices are greatly impacted by the volatility of the associated asset prices because greater volatility translates in a higher chance that the price of the associated asset will reach or surpass the strike price on or before the expiration date of the option.

Theta

This Greek is a measure of the sensitivity of the price of an option to time decay of the value of the option. Time decay describes the rate of deterioration in the value of the contract because of the passage of time. The closer the expiration date becomes, the more time decay accelerates because the time left to gain a profit narrows. Therefore, the longer it takes to reach an options' expiration date, the more value this option has because it has a longer time period to gain the trader a profit. The theta is a negative figure because time is always a diminishing factor. This figure becomes increasingly negative; the closer the expiration date becomes.

Gamma

This Greek measures the rate of change of the delta of an option. At its most basic, it tells the likelihood of an option reaching or surpassing the strike price.

Rho

This Greek is a measure of an option's value compared to changes in interest rates. Options with longer expiration dates are more likely to be affected by changes in interest rates.

The Rule for Success #10 – Be Flexible

Many options day traders find it difficult to try trading styles and strategies that they are not familiar with. While the saying of, "Do not fix it if it is not broken," is quite true, you will never become more effective and efficient in this career if you do not step out of your comfort zone at least once in a while. Yes, stick with wanting work, but allow a room for the consideration that there may be better alternatives.

The Rule for Success #11 – Have an Accountability Partner or Mentorship

Day trading options can be a rather solitary career. That means it becomes easier to sleep in if the urge strikes or just not put in a day of work. While there is nothing wrong with doing that when you have established a solid career in day trading options, this is a slippery slope that can become a harmful habit to your career. Having an accountability partner is an easy way to keep you on track with your trading plan and goals. It keeps you consistent with your actions. This can be a fellow trader, your spouse or romantic partners, a friend or family member.

Finding a mentor is also a great way to incorporate accountability as well as learning in your career.

Chapter Summary

There is more to options day trading than just having a style or a strategy. The factor that makes all the difference in whether or not the options day trader will thrive or not is the options day trader himself or herself. Dedication, hard work, and having a solid trading plan are given rules for seeking success in this career, but they are not the only ones. Other rules for success as an options day trader include:

- Having realistic expectations.
- Testing the day trading options waters by starting small and gradually increasing your operations.
- Knowing your limits so that you do not overtrade or undertrade.
- Caring for yourself mentally, emotionally, and physically so that you perform your best every day.
- Doing your homework every day with pre-market preparation.
- Analyzing your performance at the end of every options trading day.
- Not being greedy and carefully researching and analyzing positions before entering them.
- Using market volatility to your advantage.

- Using the Greeks of delta, vega, theta, gamma and rho to perform the calculations that will help you decide on how to proceed with option positions.
- Being flexible.
- Having an accountability partner or seeking a mentor.

Conclusion

Options day traders are not born. They are made, molded by hard work, dedication and persistence. The unfortunate truth is that many people come into this with stars in their eyes and greed in their hearts. They have convinced themselves that this is an easy way to make money quick, and while it is very possible for that to become a reality, this mindset approach to options day trading is not sustainable. In fact, if this person has been able to win at the beginning of this career, this approach will likely lead to this person losing all that he or she had profited.

To have long-term success as an options day trader, you need to come in with goals and a plan to back those goals. Any and everything else is possible with that trading plan. This is your business plan because options day trading is a business. It is not a hobby or something that you should do on a side in the long-term. You need to give this the times and dedication it needs to grow and thrive – just like any other business.

You have reached all the way to the end of this book, and I hope that you see the potential to make this your career. If you are still unsure if this is the career for you, here is a list of characteristics that make or break an options day trader career.

Characteristics of a Successful Options Day Trader

- Develops an options day trading system to be effective and strategic about entering and exiting positions.
- Trades in the right markets.
- Realizes that this is not a 100% foolproof method of investments. Therefore, this person plans for losses and ensures that he or she only invests in options money that he or she can afford to lose.
- Accepts losses as part of the trade and so does not dwell on the loss itself and focuses on the lesson that can be learned from the loss.
- It does not overtrade as this can place an entire portfolio at risk. Instead, a successful trader knows how to target potentially profitable opportunities.
- Does not rush into trades and instead, does proper research and analysis first.
- Uses trading styles and strategies that work for him or her individually and does not force others that do not fit his or her personality.

- Has patience and realizes that profit is not yielded the very second that a position is opened.
- Has the ability to adapt by keeping pace with the fast-changing financial market and adjusting strategies and positions to profit.
- It does not give into analysis paralysis and instead, makes sound decisions based on the current positions to execute the action.
- Knows how to create a work/life balance and knows that taking time off will benefit his or her options day trading business.
- Is open to continuous learning.

Do you have what it takes to be a successful options day trader? Can you cultivate the mindset necessary to sustain such a career? I hope that you answer yes because the financial market is rich with opportunities for people who know how to reach out and grab such opportunities.

Final Words

Congratulations on reaching the end of this book. It shows real dedication on your part to exploring options day trading as a career for you. In closing, let us quickly recap. An option is a financial contract that facilitates the right to buy or sell an asset by a certain date at a specific price called the expiration date for a certain price called a strike price.

The contract is named an option because the holder of the contract is under no obligation to exercise this right by the date specified. Options are not to be confused with stocks, which are a representation of ownership in an individual company. Stocks are an example of an asset that can be associated with an option.

Options day traders open option positions at the beginning of the day and close them by the end of the day. This is a full-time, challenging career that can be highly lucrative when done right. Benefits of day trading options include:

- Affordability as trading options is significantly lower priced than other major forms of investment, like buying stock.
- Having no obligation to buy or sell anything unless it is beneficial to do so.
- Having the ability to build a diverse portfolio.
- Having the ability to gain profit from assets owned.
- Being sustainable.

The two main types of options are called call options and put options. Call options give the trader of the option the right to buy the associated asset on or before the expiration date. Put options give the trader the right to sell the asset attached to the contract at the strike price on or before the expiration date. These two types of options can further be divided into whether or not the seller owns the associated asset.

How an options day trader chooses to pursue an option position depends on his or her trading style and how he or she does technical analysis, refers to price charts, and other reference tools. Popular options trading strategies include:

- Covered Call Strategy.
- Credit Spreads.
- Debit Spreads.
- Iron Condor.
- Rolling Out Options.
- Straddle Strategy.
- Strangle Strategy.

No matter what strategy or combination of strategies that an options day trader chooses to pursue, it all starts with:

- Practicing proper money management and risk management.
- Ensuring that risks and rewards are balanced.
- Having an effective trading strategy.
- Working with the right brokerage firm for you.
- Having realistic expectations.
- Growing your career over time with practical steps rather than big, moves that are not thought out.
- Ensuring that exits are automated.
- Doing your homework and doing pre-market preparation daily.
- Being flexible, patient, hard-working and dedicated.

As an options day trader who has found massive success, I recommend this career to anyone who wants a challenge and a job that has no limits.

Do not take on this career out of greed. Love of options trading is necessary for success. You have to love performing trades. You have to love learning techniques and strategies. You have to love keeping abreast as to what is going on, in the financial markets and on the news globally. You have to love technical analysis and reading charts. You have to love applying power principles. There is much to love about day trading options as long as you are in this for the right reasons.

I wrote this book to reach out to the person who has an analytical mind, who has big dreams and is willing to put in the work to make those dreams come true. The knowledge imparted in this book is a great jump point for your new career. Do not stop here. Learn more. Read more books. Watch videos and listen to podcasts. Find a mentor. Most importantly, do the work strategically to reap the rewards. Good luck!

From the same Author

Options Trading Crash Course

The Most Complete Guide for Beginners with Easy-To-Follow Strategies for Creating a Powerful Passive Income Stream in 2020 Using Options

Rich M. R. (2020 april)

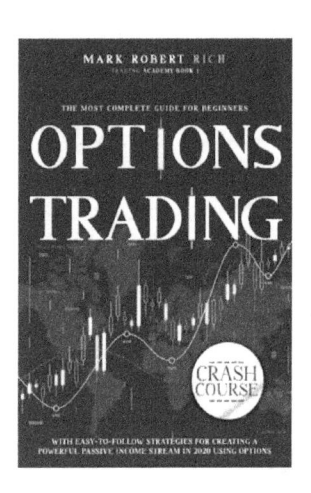

Stock Market Investing for Beginners

Complete Guide to the Stock Market with Strategies for Income Generation from ETF, Day Trading, Options, Futures, Forex, Cryptocurrencies, and More

Rich M. R. (2020 may)

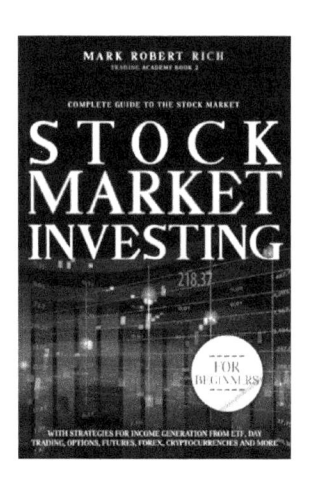

CPSIA information can be obtained
at www.ICGtesting.com
Printed in the USA
LVHW010208211120
672009LV00006B/623